What is Enlightenment?

Theories about Knowing Yourself Beneath Your Societal Identity, God and the Unseen Realm

From
Plato - Isaac Newton -
Jean-Jacques Rousseau - Immanuel Kant

by

K. J. Cleveland

Pristine Publishing

Printed 2012 by CreateSpace

This book is printed by CreateSpace. For additional copies, please visit:
www.Amazon.com

WEBSITES associated with K.J. Cleveland
www.DreamsComeTrue1.org
www.NeverGiveup1.com
www.WhatIsEnlightenment1.org
www.ToKnowThyself.org

First Printing: September 2012

ISBN-13: 978-1479392209
ISBN-10: 1479392200

Publisher: Pristine Publishing
Manhattan Beach, CA

Printed in the United States of America.

FIRST EDITION 2012

To my Brother, who has had
many wonderful conversations with me
about the theories in this book.
With love, Kelli

What is Enlightenment?

Theories about Knowing Yourself Beneath Your Societal Identity, God and the Unseen Realm From Plato, Isaac Newton, Jean-Jacques Rousseau and Immanuel Kant

Table of Contents

An Introduction

"It is the magician's bargain: give up our soul, get power in return. But once our souls, that is, our selves, have been given up, the power thus conferred will not belong to us. We shall in fact be slaves and puppets of that to which we have given our souls."
C.S. Lewis,
The Abolition of Man

"All is possible. No matter how odd wish it, and what is needed will be put in front of you to make it happen."
Lewis Carroll,
Alice in Wonderland

An Introduction

" *A*nswering the Question:
What Is Enlightenment?" is a short piece written by
Immanuel Kant in 1784. It is a profound and candid
explanation of
the importance
of being your
own self, and
thinking for
yourself. He
describes this
as a state of

> *Over 2,000 years ago Plato suggested*
> *that there was something special*
> *about each individual;*
> *that there was something magical*
> *that lay within each of us,*
> *something that gives us happiness,*
> *knowledge, and the key to the world.*
> *That magical something is our soul.*

enlightenment. Kant explains that; "Enlightenment is
man's release from his self-incurred tutelage. Tutelage is
man's inability to make use of his understanding without
direction from another. Self-incurred is this tutelage
when its cause lies not in lack of reason but in lack of
resolution and courage to use it without direction from
another...Have courage to use your own enlightenment..."

Over 2,000 years ago Plato suggested that there was
something special about each individual; that there was
something magical that lay within each of us, something
that gives us happiness, knowledge, and the key to the
world. That magical something is our soul. He said that
so many people are caught up in the world around them,

3

"I feel that I have a soul: I know it both from thought and sentiment: I know that it exists, without knowing its essence." Jean-Jacques Rousseau, "Profession of Faith of a Savoyard Vicar"

that it is as if they are chained within a cave with reality being so distant and blurred that it can only be seen as shadows on a wall.

Throughout the years many other philosophers

and physicists, including Jean-Jacques Rousseau, Immanuel Kant, Isaac Newton, and Albert Einstein, have repeatedly suggested the same thing. They say that to find peace, comfort, passion and happiness; people must look inside and get to know themselves -- their soul; and that within ourselves lay limitless knowledge about what we cannot see or touch in the physical world.

Our soul exists somewhere that is beyond empirical reasoning. Many believe this is where God resides. Others simply call it the Other World.

This book examines these theories and suggests ways to help everyone turn away from just seeing shadows on a cave to seeing full reality; to seeing ourselves and our soul.

If you're happy, you want others to be happy. If you look in your soul and find your true self, then you can get to know yourself and become happy with yourself. When you get to know yourself, you see that none of us are perfect and at the same time you begin to understand how

> *Our soul exists somewhere that is beyond empirical reasoning. Many believe this is where God resides. Others simply call it the Other World.*

to strive to be good. You'll learn to feel happy with what's in your life right now, while striving for your goals. You'll understand what true passion is. You'll learn how to have passion in all areas of your life, because it's just exciting to become you, and to develop who you are in the physical world. You'll feel true happiness instead of constant discontent. You'll find true comfort with yourself, because you know yourself, rather than pretending or trying to be something you're not.

We are all born with an instinct to survive and to become all we can be. We are born with a deep knowing and understanding of who we are and where we want to go. As we grow, our vision of ourselves can become clouded.

The words, language, communication from the people around us, how our language is structured, and how we are taught clouds a deeper understanding of who we are. Those instincts, nature, God, and the universe want to communicate with us. Our true self wants to communicate with our societal self. Our true self is who we are at birth and from nature, and our societal self is who we have learned to become in society. There is a part of us deep down that knows who we are, where we want to go, and what we want to do, but external words, symbols, and language is covering it up and blocking it out.

> *We are all born with an instinct to survive and to become all we can be. We are born with a deep knowing and understanding of who we are and where we want to go.*

This knowing communicates with us through feelings. If you neglect your internal self, you feel unhappy and unfulfilled. If you don't know your internal self, you may feel lonely. If you meet a soul mate, you feel love. If you

"…make conscious selection of that which you wish to become, it will eventually show forth in your life."
Frederick Bailes,
Hidden Power for Human Problems

follow your path, you feel fulfilled.

Our true self is who we are at our core. It is who we are at birth. It is who we are before we are taught to be different, and who we are at the root of ourselves. Throughout life those instincts, that internal self, nature, God, the universe becomes a mystery, something beyond our understanding. What we attached ourselves to is an illusion of ourselves. We can learn a great deal and do a lot of good in society, but only knowing our societal selves can cause us unhappiness when we do not also communicate with what is real deep inside us and what is original and real in nature and the universe. When you learn to listen to those instincts, those hunches; when you start to communicate with your internal self, with God, the universe, you will find your path and you will be happy. Your instincts will also protect you. That is what discovering yourself is. It is getting back to who you really are, your original self. And by doing this, you will not only find a deep peace and happiness within yourself, but also with the world around you.

Chapter 1:
Unmasking Nature:
Knowing Thyself Within a Societal Context

*"If we could be contented with being what
we are, we should have no inducement to
lament our fate; but we inflict on ourselves
a thousand real evils in seeking after an
imaginary happiness."*
Jean-Jacques Rousseau,
"Profession of Faith of a Savoyard Vicar"

"If only freedom is granted,
enlightenment is almost sure to follow."
Immanuel Kant,
"What is Enlightenment?"

Unmasking Nature:

Knowing Thyself Within a Societal Context

*I*magine you helped the government imprison a drug lord; and as a result, the government placed you in the witness protection program. They gave you a new name, job, place to live, age, and background. They gave you a whole new identity. One evening you awake in the middle of the night and look in the mirror. Are you still you? You may suffer from psychological problems because you have a new identity, but you are still the exact same person and soul. You did not vanish, and in your place exists some new entity. You are the same person with the exact same soul. You are the same person looking out of your eyes into the mirror. This is you *in nature*. And your identity, as you understand it to be, is you *in society*.

Philosophers for ages have encouraged each of us to "know thyselves." Who exactly is this person we are supposed to know? And why does it matter? I hope to clarify more concisely exactly who this person is. In order to do this, I define nature and society, and present methods of how to distinguish between you (you in nature) and your societal identity (you in society); and show you how to perceive this person within our societal context. Furthermore, I discuss how you can know thyself in nature by thinking for yourself. And that along with this self-knowledge comes clearer knowledge of the world around us, which includes perceiving nature as the fundamental reality original to society. And finally if people know themselves through nature, they will become what Immanuel Kant and Plato refer to as enlightened. Finally, I surmise how people know themselves, think for themselves, and become enlightened is done within nature and beyond society. To simplify I define society as being anything created by humans, and nature as anything not created by humans. [1]

Nature = Anything _NOT_ created by humans.

Society = Anything created by humans.

What is Nature?

First, I will define what I mean by nature and you in nature. You in nature is the you without societal labels. You are who you are inside yourself, your soul. You are who you are outside society. You from nature is not your income, your name, your profession, your social status, or where you live. Therefore, you cannot be anything created by society.

"...whatever religion you may ultimately embrace, remember that its real duties are independent of human institutions-that no religion upon earth can dispense with the sacred obligations of morality-that an upright heart is the temple of the Divinity..."
Jean-Jacques Rousseau,
"Profession of Faith of a Savoyard Vicar"

Isaac Newton gives an example of nature as being a "respiration in a man and in a beast, the descent of stones in Europe and in America, the light of our culinary fire and of the sun, the reflection of light in the earth and in the planets." Newton discovered gravity, or that something not created by humans keeps us on Earth. He understood it as being a force that holds us to

To Know Thyself

Imagine you helped the government imprison a drug lord; and as a result, the government placed you in the witness protection program. They gave you a new name, job, place to live, age, and background. They gave you a whole new identity. One evening you awake in the middle of the night and look in the mirror. Are you still you? You may suffer from psychological problems because you have a new identity, but you are still the exact same person and soul. You did not vanish, and in your place exists some new entity. You are the same person with the exact same soul. You are the same person looking out of your eyes into the mirror. This is you *in nature*. And your identity, as you understand it to be, is you *in society*.

Philosophers for ages have encouraged each of us to "know thyselves."

1. Who exactly is this person you are beneath your societal identity?
2. If you look deep within yourself, what kind of person does it feel good to be? What do you really like? Who do you really want to be?

"What lies behind us and what lies before us are tiny matters compared to what lies within us."
Oliver Wendell Holmes

the Earth, though he could not uncover the source of this force. Nevertheless, gravity is an example of nature along with many things physicists study. Furthermore, you and your soul are a part of nature.[2]

"Nature, my dear youth, hath hitherto in this respect been silent in you," explained the teacher in Jean-Jacques Rousseau's "Profession of Faith of the Savoyard Vicar." Nature is also you. You were created by nature, your mind and your soul are a part of nature. Rousseau

"Enlightenment is man's release from his self-incurred tutelage. Tutelage is man's inability to make use of his understanding without direction from another. Self-incurred is this tutelage when its cause lies not in lack of reason but in lack of resolution and courage to use it without direction from another...Have courage to use your own enlightenment..."
Immanuel Kant,
"What is Enlightenment?"

believed that within ourselves exists a world of knowledge written by nature, and admonishes people who do not look inward at their nature: "Remember that you offend her more by anticipating her instructions than by refusing to hear them."[3]

"You are your own RAW material. When you know what you consist of and what you want to make of it then you can invent yourself."
Warren G. Bennis

What is Society?

Secondly, I will define what I mean by society and knowing you in society, (which I call your societal identity.) By society, I mean everything in our world that has been created by humans. For example, mental creations by humans include language or verbal communication, doctrines, belief systems, the ability to read and write; physical creations include buildings, highways, churches, temples, and school systems. All of these things form society. Nature is what

> "Nature, my dear youth, hath hitherto in this respect been silent in you," explained the teacher in Jean-Jacques Rousseau's "Profession of Faith of the Savoyard Vicar." Nature is also you. You were created by nature, your mind and your soul are a part of nature.

exists beneath all of this. With technology and our intricate social structure ubiquitously surrounding us, it may be more challenging for humans to perceive nature.

People's societal identity is how they have come to define themselves since birth. Their societal identity is what can change. People can change their name, their career, and their belief system. They can change what represents them, their identity, but they cannot change *who they are*. Kant and Plato may argue that for people to see themselves as the sum of their societal identity is to lose the essence of who they really are, which decreases perception or enlightenment of the real world around them.

In the *Allegory of the Cave*, I interpret Plato as meaning that the cave is an allegory of society, and that the people in the cave, who only perceive what is in front of them without seeing nature and the rest of the world, are chained. Plato says; "Can human beings living in a cave, which has a mouth

"Sow a thought and you reap an action; sow an act and you reap a habit; sow a habit and you reap a character; sow a character and you reap a destiny."
Ralph Waldo Emerson

open toward the light? Here they have been from their childhood and have their legs and necks chained so they cannot move. They can only see in front of them, being prevented by the chains from turning their heads around." They are chained to

Plato further says,
"When any of them is liberated
and suddenly compelled to stand up and turn around
and walk and look toward the light,
he will suffer sharp pains.
The glare will hurt him
and he will be unable to see
the realities of which,
in his former state,
he has only seen the shadows.
Then imagine someone says to him
what he saw before was an illusion;
but now, when he is approaching nearer to reality
and his eye is turned toward more real existence,
he has a clearer vision."

what they are taught; society is their only reality. They are chained and kept from turning their heads to see all that exists around them. Plato continues; "above the walkway like the screen which puppet players have in front of them, over which they show the puppets."4

Their perception is only a shadow of reality, and

"One can go back toward safety or forward toward growth."
Abraham Maslow

they are like puppets bound to this perception created by society. Plato explains that the allegory is "Like ourselves, and they see only their own shadows, or the shadows of one another, which the fire throws on the opposite wall of the cave." The people in Plato's cave only see shadows of objects, all created by man, which includes more than objects, such as social institutions. They see a shadow of an image created by society, and this is their reality. For example, most children are raised with

> "If I have a book which understands for me, a pastor who has a conscience for me, a physician who decides my diet, and so forth, I need not trouble myself. I need not think, if I can only pay-others will readily undertake the irksome work for me."
>
> Immanuel Kant
> "What is Enlightenment?"

particular ethnic or cultural views. If that's all children see, they will come to see their cultural view as reality, rather than seeing the big picture, that their culture is created by society. "To them the truth would be literally nothing but the shadows of images," Plato observes.5

Plato further says, "When any of them is liberated and suddenly compelled to stand up and turn around and walk and look toward the light, he will suffer sharp pains. The glare will hurt him and he

"As one grows in his sense of the inner beauty of things he comes to a place where he knows whether any act is in line with his sense of beauty or not. If it is not, he will give it up himself without being told, and will feel no clinging to it. His inner self comes to know truth, goodness, and beauty to be the highest values; these values are eternal in the human race."
Frederick Bailes,
Hidden Power for Human Problems

will be unable to see the realities of which, in his former state, he has only seen the shadows. Then imagine someone says to him what he saw before was an illusion; but now, when he is approaching nearer to reality and his eye is turned toward more real existence, he has a clearer vision."[6]

However, the problem with seeing reality for the first

time is that "When he approaches the sunlight his eyes will be dazzled, and he will not be able to see anything at all of what are now called realities." Therefore, Plato surmises; " That he will need to grow accustomed to the sight of the upper world. And first he will see shadows best, next the reflections of men and other objects in the water, and then the objects themselves....Last of all he will be able to see the sun and not mere reflections of it in the water..." Plato calls this process "the ascent of the soul in to the world of Forms..." And that "the power and capacity of learning exists in the soul..."7

You and the Creation of Your Societal Identity

Next, why is knowing thyself, knowing you from nature, along with knowing your societal identity important? Because it is the source of where people make decisions from their own point of view. If they never make decisions from their own frame of reference and have only made decisions based on what they have learned in society, then they only know what society has presented to them; and thus do not know themselves. And if they do not know themselves, then they cannot feel full peace, passion, happiness and comfort with their selves. Kant argues in *What is Enlightenment?* that "if I have a book which provides meaning for me, a pastor who has conscience for me, a doctor who will judge my diet for me and so on, then I do not need to exert myself. I

"But we sometimes confuse naivete and inno-cence. We may think it is mature to be cyni-cal and immature to be innocent."
Thomas Moore,
Original Self

do not have any need to think..." People need to think for themselves in order to know themselves; and if cul-ture and society is making their decisions for them, then they do not know themselves.[8]

When you are born, you have experiences that shape who you become in life. If humans created society, then language is the basis of civilization. With verbal communication, society was created. Meanings of words shape how we perceive things, and sentences shape how we understand things. Language is important because it is the core of how we came into existence, and how we became as advanced as we are today.

> Because as soon as people gained that consciousness of themselves, of being able to recognize themselves in the mirror, they started building structures and institutions in society that bound them from recognizing that consciousness.

Through the use of language, people can be conditioned to become what society teaches them to be. They may be taught to view the world externally, and create their societal identity based on what they find there. They may not even recognize that they may have lost sight of their real selves from nature; and therefore, their societal identity becomes intrinsically important in defining who they are. They attach themselves to that creation as being who they really are. They perceive the world through their experiences alone. And thus, the gift of consciousness given to us when we learned to speak becomes a cage. Leakey explains: "for language and reflective self-awareness are undoubtedly a closely linked phenomena." Because as soon as people gained that consciousness of themselves, of being able to recognize themselves in the mirror, they

"Make visible what, without you,
might perhaps never have been seen."
Robert Biessen

started building structures and institutions in society
that bound them from recognizing that consciousness.[9]

With verbal and nonverbal discourse we are taught
how to survive. Parents and teachers and all grown ups
who came into our young world, said things like: "hoe a
plant this way to make it grow better," or "preserve meat
with salt it makes it last longer." These basic things help
us grow more quickly without having to figure it out our-

selves. We absorbed the information. We learn they are right, by rebelling or trying it out.

With the creation of civilization and the spoken language, people develop an awareness and a higher intelligence of themselves and the world. But with the very thing that may have given people enlightenment is exactly what they used to build the societal illusions that mask the realness and awareness they received. Richard Leakey pointed out: "There is no question that the evolution of spoken language as we know it was a defining point of human prehistory. Perhaps it was *the* defining point. Equipped with language, humans were able to create new kinds of worlds in nature: the world of introspective consciousness and the world we manufacture and share with others, which we call 'culture.'"[10]

Kant explains that in order for people to free themselves and therefore know themselves, they must learn to "use one's intelligence without the guidance of another." He believes that it is not the lack of intelligence that keeps us from being guided by other people in society, but it is the lack of determination and courage.

My argument is that when philosophers and other people refer to "knowing thyselves," it is "thyself" that we were aware of at the same time we created language, before we built societal identities on top of that person.

"If you're going to succeed at being yourself, you're going to have to focus on your potential-what God has created you to be-not your limitations."

Joyce Meyer

It is the self-awareness and consciousness of ourselves, the future, mortality and our fragility. For example, animals were never given this type of awareness. They are only who they are from nature, their soul; and they are never a societal identity. If we know ourselves, we can

Kant suggests that once people acclimate to being only their societal identity, they typically fear becoming their own selves; "After having made their domestic animals dumb and having carefully prevented these quiet creatures from daring to take any step beyond the lead-strings to which they have fastened them, these guardians then show them the danger which threatens them, should they attempt to walk alone. Now this danger is not really so very great; for they would presumably learn to walk after some stumbling. However, an example of this kind intimidates and frightens people out of all further attempts."

create a societal identity that is an outthrust of ourselves and not merely an example, a shell, of the culture or society in which we live. For example, Rousseau explains that just as a deaf man may "deny the reality of sounds, because his ears were never sensible of them," that people who do not know themselves deny that they exist beyond a societal identity because they do not look inward and see themselves. Leakey also suggests: "We are so very

much a product of the culture that shaped us that we often fail to recognize it as an artifact of our own making, until we are faced with a very different culture." Therefore, in order for people to know themselves in nature, they must first think for themselves.[11]

Finally, if nature is anything not created by man, then that not only includes the forest, lakes, trees, animals and reptiles; but it also includes our conscious and subconscious mind. What goes on in our mind is not tangible, but it is from nature. People can get lost in their societal world and come to believe that who they are in society is who they really are.

"Freedom is not just a dream...it's there...on the other side of the fences we build all by ourselves." From the movie Instinct

Thinking for Yourself Gets You Back to Nature

Kant explains that in order for people to free themselves and therefore know themselves, they must learn to "use one's intelligence without the guidance of another." He believes that it is not the lack of intelligence that keeps us from being guided by other people in society, but it is the lack of determination and courage. He further explains that "even after nature has freed them from alien guidance," people gladly remain imprisoned. They would rather have other people be their guide than to think for themselves. Kant suggests that once people acclimate to being only their societal identity, they typically fear becoming their own selves; "After having made their domestic animals dumb and having carefully prevented these quiet creatures from daring to take any step beyond the lead-strings to which they have fastened them, these guardians then show them the danger which threatens them,

"That's the way things come clear all of sudden. And then you realize how obvious they've been all along."
Makeleine L'Engle

should they attempt to walk alone. Now this danger is not really so very great; for they would presumably learn to walk after some stumbling. However, an example of this kind intimidates and frightens people out of all further attempts." He explains that this way of life has become so natural to them and it is challenging to work them selves out of this situation. Typically, people become fond of this situation and get used to not thinking for them selves because they have never actually done it; and thus, relying on others to think for them becomes the "ankle-chains of a perpetual minority." He believes that freedom is all that is required for this enlightenment.[12]

Knowing Thyself and Enlightenment

How does knowing thyself bring about enlightenment? It is a gaining of knowledge where people feel like they wake up and see the world for the first time. It is described as coming out of a comatose state and attaining broader knowledge of their environment. Those newly enlightened people no longer feel hypnotized and are suddenly aware of themselves. When the veil is removed, they open their eyes and see so much more than simple illusions of reality. Society isn't an illusion,

> How does knowing thyself bring about enlightenment? It is a gaining of knowledge where people feel like they wake up and see the world for the first time.

but if we do not see the big picture, we have an
illusion of ourselves and the world. Because by
only seeing the world through societies' eyes, we
may think that all these things will make us happy
but they will not. But by seeing the world from our
souls, we have a better idea of how to truly be
happy.

> *Knowing thyself is important for many*
>
> *reasons, but fundamentally*
>
> *people acknowledging who they*
>
> *really are gives them autonomy over their life to*
>
> *a greater extent.*

What is required to attain enlightenment?
Consciousness gained with the creation of the spoken language was lost when people built society,
civilization and culture. People became so closely
tied to society and their societal identity that they
came to see it as the sum of who they are; and

thus, veiled their original selves. Therefore, by knowing thyself, a person can be enlightened once again.

Why It is Important

Knowing thyself is important for many reasons, but fundamentally people acknowledging who they really are gives them autonomy over their life to a greater extent. The reason is because if people notice fully that society is created, rather than inherent from birth or nature, then they have more power to shape and form their societal identity or who they want to be in society. The reason I say more power rather than the power is because people are still influenced by their culture in becoming

*"We are born naïve, but we can grow
into innocence..."*
Thomas Moore,
Original Self

who they are, but they will no longer be blindly
following a herd.

Understanding these concepts are important
individually because people learn to define themselves as more than their societal identity and
realize that they can become who they want in

society. They do not feel their societal identity limits who they are and what they can become. Society can be a gift for them. For example, if a young woman, who lives in Manhattan and drives a Mercedes, believes that her car or her income defines her, then she may feel so attached to that identity that she may never move beyond that station in life and become

While writing the Letter from the Birmingham Jail, Martin Luther King said it was necessary for individuals to "rise from the bondage of myths and half-truths to the unfettered realm of creative analysis and objective appraisal..."

all that could make her happy. By only seeing herself as what she is and not who she is, she imprisons herself. She does not see the forest (nature) for the trees (her society).

Furthermore, understanding these concepts is important for more than just individual reasons. For example, religion was created in society to help us get closer to God; however, some people are so strongly attached to their own religion that they have waged wars, and forgotten the true importance of why we have those religions to begin with, which is to love God and others, and to be good people. Another example is Martin Luther King and the civil rights movement. He argued that people should look beyond race, or the color of our skin, and realize that we are all humans, only altered by our skin color and what our culture has

taught us to become. While writing the *Letter from the Birmingham Jail*, Martin Luther King said it was necessary for individuals to "rise from the bondage of myths and half-truths to the unfettered realm of creative analysis and objective appraisal..."[13]

Arguments against My Claim

Some people may argue that humans can create nature because scientists now have the ability to clone. However, they only have the ability to initiate a new being, not the actual creation of it. They only know how to spawn the process, but then the cells, which they did not create, start creating the new being. The replica DNA was not created by society, scientists only start the process in order to get the cells to start reproducing as they have always done. They did not create the DNA, or the cell, and they do not actually make the being. Therefore, the being is only reproduced genetically; it is not actually built by society.

And although people may be attached to this person created within society, they are still themselves beneath their societal identity. A societal identity can represent people, or represent what others want them to be. Their societal identity can change radically, but they are still the exact same person with the same soul.

Others may argue that people are fundamentally their societal identity, and that they are their name, their career, their religious affiliation, or their belief system. And that society is a real and an accurate perception of the world. But I counter that people's societal identity is a creation and can change, and it can be an extension of themselves or it can be a shell simply created by society alone. And although people may be attached to this person created within society, they are still themselves beneath their societal identity. A societal identity

can represent people, or represent what others want them to be. Their societal identity can change radically, but they are still the exact same person with the same soul.

The example used at the beginning of the paper about people losing their societal identity when put into the witness protection program clear-

> *With a whole new identity, they are still exactly the same person.*

ly defines who you really are within nature. Like I said before, when people are put into the witness protection program and given a whole new identity, they do not vanish and in their place exists a new person, with a new mind, and a new soul. They still remember the same experiences they had with their previous identity. It was still you who went to that

school, lived in that house, and so forth. With a
whole new identity, they are still exactly the same
person. Memory is the proof that we have a very
real soul beyond our societal identity, but it is not
required to prove a soul exists. Because even people with amnesia have the same soul and body, but
have just forgotten their past. People are who they
are without the social labels that created what the
witness protection program changed. They are the
you inside themselves. Some may call this your
soul, Rousseau explains: "I feel I have a soul: I
know it both from thoughts and sentiment: I know
that it exists, without knowing its essence."
Rousseau retorts that just as a deaf man may argue
that because he can not hear sounds they do not

"It takes courage to grow up and turn out to be who you really are."
E. E. Cummings

exist, people who do not know themselves are "deaf to that internal voice which, nevertheless, calls to them so loud and emphatically."[14]

Conclusion

Looking inward is essential for you to discover who you are. You are who you are outside society. The you from nature is not your name, your profession, your income, your social status, or where you live. If you lost all these things, you would still be the exact same person looking into the mirror.

Your mind proves this in that you remember, "and that to be in fact the same person, I must remember to have previously existed."[15]

When given the power to really decide who you want to be in society, you will feel free. If you want, your societal identity can be an out-thrust of your wishes, desires and beliefs from the real you in nature. Society can be a gift and a tool that gives you the freedom to become all you want in society. As Kant states, "Therefore nature has cherished, within its hard shell, the germ of the inclination and need for free thought. This free thought gradually acts upon the mind of the people and they gradually become more capable of acting in freedom."[16]

> As Kant states, "Therefore nature has cherished, within its hard shell, the germ of the inclination and need for free thought. This free thought gradually acts upon the mind of the people and they gradually become more capable of acting in freedom."

In the next chapter, I present a table distinguishing the Other World (which I tend to refer to as also the nature we cannot sense with our five senses), nature that we can see and sense, and society. It is deduced from Immanuel Kant's *Critique of Pure Reason*. Once we get to know ourselves, it is important to understand where we came from or from where we were created. In order to do that, I learned about nature and/or the Other World. I find it helpful to look at the table in order to wrap my head around how society comes from physical nature, which comes from nature in the Other World, or the *A Priori*. It helps me understand and

remember where I originated. I came from something beyond my physical experiences. I have beliefs about what is there, though I can't physically prove it. But I can sense my soul there with a means other than my five senses, and some sort of knowledge beyond me. I feel the peace, understanding and love there. I know that within it lies the source of good in life.[17]

Endnotes:

1 See Plato, *A Guided Tour of Five Works by Plato*, translated and edited by Christopher Biffle, (Mountain View, CA: Mayfield Publishing, 2001), 83-86, and Kant, Immanuel, *Basic Writings of Kant*, edited and with a Foreword by Allen W. Wood, (New York: Modern Library, 2001), 135.

2 Isaac Newton, *Newton's Philosophy of Nature*, Edited and with a Foreword by H. S. Thayer, (New York: Hafner Press, 1953), 3.

3 Jean-Jacques Rousseau, *The Harvard Classics: French and English Philosopher*, "Profession of Faith of the Savoyard Vicar, (New York: P. F. Collier, 1910), 240.

4 Plato, *A Guided Tour of Five Works by Plato*, translated and edited by Christopher Biffle, (Mountain View, CA: Mayfield Publishing, 2001), 83-86.

5 Ibid.

6 Ibid.

7 Ibid.

8 Kant, Immanuel, *Basic Writings of Kant*, edited and with a Foreword by Allen W. Wood, (New York: Modern Library, 2001), 135.

9 Richard Leakey, *The Origin of Humankind*, (New York: Basic Books, 1994), 141.

10 Richard Leakey, *The Origin of Humankind*, (New York: Basic Books, 1994), 119.

11 See Jean-Jacques Rousseau, *The Harvard Classics: French and English Philosopher*, "Profession of Faith of the Savoyard Vicar, (New York: P. F. Collier, 1910), 258 and Richard Leakey, *The Origin of Humankind*, (New York: Basic

Books, 1994), 121.

12 Kant, Immanuel, *Basic Writings of Kant*, edited and with a Foreword by Allen W. Wood, (New York: Modern Library, 2001), 135-6.

13 Gary E. Kessler, *Voices of Wisdom: A Multicultural Philosophy Reader*, (Belmont, CA: Thomson Learning), 175.

14 Jean Jacques Rousseau, *The Harvard Classics: French and English Philosopher*, "Profession of Faith of the Savoyard Vicar, (New York: P. F. Collier, 1910), 259 & 264.

15 Ibid, 264.

16 Kant, Immanuel, *Basic Writings of Kant*, edited and with a Foreword by Allen W. Wood, (New York: Modern Library, 2001), 141.

17 Kant, Immanuel, *Critique of Pure Reason*, translated by Norman Kemp Smith, (New York: Bedford/St. Martins, 1965).

Chapter 2:
Kant's *A Priori*:
A Table of the Other World

"I perceive the deity in all his works, I feel him within me, and behold him in every object around me..."
Jean Jacques Rousseau,
"Profession of Faith of a Savoyard Vicar"

Kant's *A Priori*:
A Table of the Other World

The following table, mostly derived from Immanuel Kant's *Critique of Pure Reason*, distinguishes between the Other World in nature, the physical world from nature, and our society. Looking at this information in a table helps me understand the source of our existence, where we all originated. Does it not make sense that the true key to happiness exist in the place in which we were created? By understanding more clearly where my soul is from, I can see better who it is within myself I am getting to know. I can see me, my soul, better. I believe that knowledge of the *A Priori* comes to us through our mind and soul. We have to look inside to see it, Kant calls it Pure Intuition. And I believe that when we see nature and society in the physical world more clearly, they become gifts.[1]

They become gifts for us to create a societal identity representing who we really are. And they become gifts for us to utilize in order to make our dreams come true, and create the life we want. I believe dreams are our soul trying to speak to us about who it is we are to truly become in life. Our goals and dreams are the source of happiness on Earth. This table helps me break down the levels of our existence, where we came from and what we created for ourselves.

50

The Unseen

A Priori: **Nature in the** **Other World**	**Nature:** **Our World** **or the** ***A Posteriori***	**Society:** **What People** **Built, also the** ***A Posteriori***
In it exists:	In it exists:	In it exists:
The language of Mathematics; Space and Time	Forests, lakes, trees, the ocean, mountains, our selves and animals; everything not created by human beings.	Language and discourse, buildings, religion, doctrines, highways, technology and everything else humans created.
God; the Creator; Intelligent Benevolent Being(s)		
Shape - Forms	What exists in our world from the *A Priori* that can be studied empirically.	Here exists all things created by society. These are things we created that we can sense with our body and our five senses.
Where our selves and our souls are created.		
What exists in the *A Priori* has no color, so we cannot sense it with our five senses.	Our five senses on the body that feed into the mind.	

The Unseen

A Priori:
Nature in the
Other World

Nature:
Our World
or the
A Posteriori

Society:
What People
Built, also the
A Posteriori

Examples of what exists in the *A Priori* are space, time, and mathematics, and they are true in nature or the Other World's creation of them.

They are things in nature we cannot sense with our body and five senses, but we may be able to sense them with our minds and our soul.

How do we sense things in the *A Priori* (such as

Some philosophers, physicists and other people believe that our mind has the *power to create.* That power inside us lay within our soul and our mind, but we create in physical nature. Our world of nature would be our canvas.

This is where we acquired an awareness of ourselves.

Here exists our *power to create*

In it exists language. We created words to mean what they mean. They are true by our creation of them.

Words are true in our creation of them to be what they are.

The Unseen

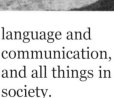

time, space, and math)?
Immanuel Kant believes it is with what he calls Pure Intuition.

We can't empirically prove anything that exists in the *A Priori*, because we cannot sense it or do experiments on it.

Space isn't empirical. We do not know space exists by empirical reasoning. We cannot touch space, or physically feel it, or see it, and hear it. We cannot sense it.

language and communication, and all things in society.

Matter and color exist here.

Within nature exists things created by whomever or whatever is in the Other World.

The Unseen

Within the *A Priori* exists Necessary Truths that are also Synthetic Truths.

Within nature exists Contingent Truths and Synthetic Truths

Within Society exists Necessary Truths, which are also Analytic Truths.

Necessary Truths - They are true independent of empirical experience.

Synthetic Truths - These are things that can change, but in the *A Priori* they do not actually change, only our understanding of them changes. They were created within the *A Priori*, not by society, and exist there. And we

Contingent Truths - Are all known to be true on the basis of experience. It is everything created in nature by what is in the *A Priori* for us to sense with our five senses. All of it can be measured.

Synthetic Truths - These can change, and we must experience them to see if they are true.

Necessary Truths - They are known to be true independent of experience.

Everything created by the what exists in the *A Priori* and by humans or society are necessary truths.

Analytic Truths - Are all things created by our society. And they are therefore necessary

The Unseen

know they are there, but not by any of our five senses. The reason we must call them synthetic truths, is because what we know and understand of them can change.

For example, three-hundred years ago, we thought that space and time were static and unchanging. However, with discoveries by Newton and Einstein we abolished the notion of absolute space and time, and thus our understanding of what

For example, to say that "Earth has one moon," is something we have to look at (experience) to make sure that it does in fact have one moon. We did not create Earth or its moon, therefore we must experience it in order to know it indeed has one moon.

If something is a contingent and synthetic truth, then it is something that exists in nature, created in nature, not by society or humans; therefore, it must be studied and

and true just in our creation of them. We basically created them to mean what they mean.

For example, to say "All unicorns have a single horn," is an analytic and necessary truth, because we created the word unicorn to mean a horse with a single horn. Society created the word "unicorn" to mean "a horse with a single horn." No experience of it is needed; it's true in the definition of the word we created.

The Unseen

A Priori:
we originally believed.

If something is a necessary and synthetic truth then it exists within the _A Priori_, and it cannot be empirically studied or measured because we can not touch, taste, smell, hear or see it. And it does not change, but our understanding of it can change. Because we did not create it, our understanding of it can change, but it doesn't actually change itself.

Nature:
measured in order to see what it will do. Fortunately, within nature things tend to have regularities.

In nature exists regularities to help us live and survive in the world. These things we can touch, taste, smell, hear and see.

We learn to survive in nature by the regularities in it, through experiencing them. We learn not to touch fire by experience, because it will

Society:
If something is a necessary and analytic truth, then it was created by us, society, humans.

Humans created our language, we built our cities; therefore, we know all the ins and outs of it. There's nothing to investigate, because we created it. However, what nature makes we must investigate, in order to understand it, because we didn't create it.

More on Nature:

repeatedly burn us, and not by initial reason. Repetition in nature, not theoretical reasoning, is necessary to study this.

We do not know why fruits and vegetables, or all food from nature or the *A Priori*, have nutrients in them, but from experience we know they do. We do not know, because we did not create them. We can break these things down and study them because we know they are going to reproduce in a regular fashion. We can imagine with our minds that fruits and vegetables, or all food not created by humans, do not have nutrients, but through study and experiments, we know they do.

We can imagine that the sky is blue, but before we saw it, we could have also imagined it being a different color; but because we regularly see that it is blue, we can study it; and thus the birth of science. Because of the regularities of nature, we are enabled with the ability to study those regularities, survive and advance in our world.

All things not created by society or human beings tend to have regularities that we can study. It is as if God, nature, or whatever exists in the Other World gave us these regularities as a way to survive in this world. Because of them, we can develop medicines, do surgeries, learn what to stay away from, because all things created here by nature tend to regularly do the same thing.

Theories of the Other World:

By unmasking nature, you may find God within it's creation. It's quite obvious if you just look; we can see that an intelligence created nature. Society's okay; nature's okay. But we can learn to see through society and what we created to what was originally there, in nature and the *A Priori*. Our soul exists in nature and the *A Priori*, before society taught us who we are and created our societal identity. We can find who we are before society taught us who to be. Why should we do this? Because fundamental happiness, peace, and passion reside here.

Why do some refuse to acknowledge what we cannot empirically study? For closed-minded or extreme scientists or academics, to acknowledge the *A Priori* means they must give up control. It means they no longer have all the answers. So they deny it exists and are blind to it, because it's too scary to accept the unknown.

And for cults or extreme religious fanatics, they believe that their religion is all that exists in the *A Priori*. It makes them feel safe to believe that, because this gives them a feeling of control over their lives and their fate. Therefore, to challenge their beliefs is just too scary and so they will kill or wage wars to protect the safety net of their belief system.

However; for many religions and people who open-mindedly study a belief system or create their own beliefs and theorize about what's in the *A Priori*, their beliefs give them the answers to what they cannot experience with their five senses. They realize many paths could exist, but they feel comfortable with their own.

"... may he be ever as happy as myself; so far from exciting jealousy, his happiness will only add to my own."

Jean-Jacques Rousseau,

"Profession of Faith of a Savoyard Vicar"

They have their own theories about what they believe exists in the Other World or the *A Priori*, and know other people's beliefs may differ, but they feel safe and more open with accepting other belief systems.

I know it is impossible to empirically prove exactly what is in the *A Priori*, but it doesn't mean we should just pretend it doesn't exist. Something does exist; and many people have some fascinating theories about what it is.

And of course I am a proponent of empirical science as well, the two aren't in binary opposition to each other. Empirical science saves our lives and helps us advance, but rational science is where theory lay, and within it we find our souls.

Regarding empiricism, our conclusions from it do not come from theoretical reasoning, but from experiencing the same thing over and over again, repeatedly; or noticing that most things in nature happen in the same way. Empiricism is studying repetition. It takes acquiring knowledge and using our intelligence in an advanced manner in order to study them effectively, but it is repetition in nature that we are studying in order to create medicine, do surgeries, save lives, and just to live a simple daily life.

What creates these regularities in nature? I know we all have our own beliefs, but strictly as far as my beliefs go, I believe it is God, or some benevolent intelligent being(s). From what has been presented and proved to me through Pure Intuition, I believe this Intelligent Being is omniscient, omnipotent, and omnipresent. And that by looking inside ourselves, we learn how to communicate with God and receive help daily. I believe we have free-will, and that who is in the Other World does not cause bad things to happen, or if so, it is for us to learn something important. Furthermore, by the process of free-will existing in this world, if bad things do happen to us, this Being will help us through them and help us learn something good from them if we ask for help. I believe we are all born with a purpose, and it is our choice to walk down that fated path. We are born with a choice to live our destined lives. I believe by not seeing what is in the *A Priori*, we are given a fundamental test of having faith in our selves and God. After all, if we could see and touch what is in the Other World, then faith would be easy. Instead we must learn to trust God and what is inside us in order to have true faith. From

"God does not play dice with the universe."
Albert Einstein

my experiences, that is what I have learned about the Other World.

Now, there is more that I choose to believe based on what I have learned in my environment. Being raised a

> If we refuse to study
> and theorize about
> the Other World
> (or the *A Priori*)
> because it is challenging
> and we may never
> empirically prove the
> ultimate cause, then we are
> just pretending it isn't there.
> And therefore, we end up
> ignoring the fact that the
> *A Priori* is probably what
> causes those regularities in
> nature that we experience
> to begin with.

Baptist and partially Methodist, my belief system is fairly related and comparable to these. I feel comfort from these beliefs. None of this has been empirically proven to me, but it is what I choose to believe. Realizing this; I therefore, have complete freedom to fully allow others to have their own beliefs. However, I do not believe anything from such a benevolent source would ever encourage anyone to hurt others as game or because their mind tells them to do it and so forth. Those people may have psychological problems or something else, but it isn't from a benevolent God or soul. These things I experienced and religious belief systems I acquired and accepted, I do not know through empirical reasoning. Will we ever know the ultimate causes of these regularities in nature? And does that mean we should pretend they do not exist?

If we refuse to study and theorize about the Other World (or the *A Priori*) because it is challenging and we may never empirically prove the ultimate cause, then we are just pretending it isn't there. And therefore, we end up ignoring the fact that the *A Priori* is probably what causes those regularities in nature that we experience to begin with.

For example, how reliable is it to only use empirical methods to learn about our history? Without intellectual theory based on evidence and what we know, we would probably have a very narrow view

> ...Jean-Jacques Rousseau said; "Let us suppose that a man, born deaf, should deny the reality of sounds, because his ears were never sensible of them." The man said; "Either make the sounds perceptible to me, or I shall continue to doubt their existence." This is true of things that exist that we cannot empirically prove, but Rousseau states that this is a specific example of what people deny within themselves. He surmised that many people are "...deaf to that internal voice which, nevertheless, calls to them so loud and emphatically."

and false idea about our past. Think of all that can be lost, burned or destroyed. Even though we could never empirically prove it existed to begin with, it would be inaccurate to just pretend it never existed. Therefore, theory combined with empirical evidence is necessary to achieve the greatest amount of truth about our pasts.

Another example, Jean-Jacques Rousseau said;

"Life begins at the end of your comfort zone."
Neale Donald Walsch

"Let us suppose that a man, born deaf, should deny the reality of sounds, because his ears were never sensible of them." The man said; "Either make the sounds perceptible to me, or I shall continue to doubt their existence." This is true of things that exist that we cannot empirically prove, but Rousseau states that this is a specific example of what people deny within themselves. He surmised that many people are "...deaf to that internal voice which, nevertheless, calls to them so loud and emphatically."[2]

In the next two chapters, I examine Isaac Newton and Jean-Jacque Rousseau's theories about the proof of God's existence. They are scientific, rational and mathematical theories about what they believe to exist in the *A Priori.*

Endnotes:

[1]Kant, Immanuel, *Critique of Pure Reason*, translated by Norman Kemp Smith, (New York: Bedford/St. Martins, 1965).

[2]Jean-Jacques Rousseau, *The Harvard Classics: French and English Philosopher*, "Profession of Faith of the Savoyard Vicar, (New York: P. F. Collier, 1910), 258-259.

Chapter 3:
Isaac Newton's
Theory of God and the Soul

"We find God through His handiwork as well as through the sacred writings."
Frederick Bailes,
Hidden Power for Human Problems.

Isaac Newton's
Theory of God and the Soul

*D*uring the seventeenth-century the emerging mechanical philosophy sought to separate the study of science from God. Most proponents of this philosophy still believed in a Deity; however, they believed He created a perfect universe and then stepped out of the picture. Isaac Newton maintained a life long profound belief in God. He believed that all the causes studied within science were created by God. After Isaac Newton wrote

Philosophiae Naturalis Principia Mathematica in 1686, he decided not all things could be explained mechanically. He believed that God created the world and then continued to help it run smoothly through divine intervention. Therefore, his philosophical interpretation of the universe determined that God and science were interdependent on each other.

It was impossible for science to mechanically determine all causes in the universe. What this means is that science could determine *how* something happened, but not *why* it happened. For example, though over-simply stated, the *big bang* theory suggests that a mass of dirt and related particles exploded and created our universe. That is an *effect*, but we have no idea what *caused* it to happen. Why would a mass of dirt explode for *no given reason* creating a perfectly orbiting universe? Scientists can prove the effects, but not what causes certain events to occur. Nor can they prove why certain things exist to begin with. Although scientific knowledge was more limited during

> ...though over-simply stated, the *big bang* theory suggests that a mass of dirt and related particles exploded and created our universe. That is an *effect*, but we have no idea what *caused* it to happen. Why would a mass of dirt explode for *no given reason* creating a perfectly orbiting universe?

Newton's time than it is now, his points were still valid. The awe-inspiring order of the world and what causes it to come into existence forced many physicists to return to the possibility of divine intervention and the connection of science and God.

"The philosophy of the seventeenth-century has often been seen as connected with a gradual march from religious orthodoxy and oppression towards pre-Enlightenment deism, agnosticism, atheism, and toleration;" Richard Popkin remarked to be a general view of how scholars have interpreted the religious movement during that time. Explanation of science had traditionally been linked with causation. To prove phenomena, scientists must be able to explain the cause. People who supported the Aristotelian systems and the mechanical philosophy of the seventeenth-century believed that explanation provided "knowledge of the cause of phenomenon." According to Spinoza, "all effects, all phenomena and events, follow with absolute necessity from the divine nature

(*Natura Naturans*)."[1]

He believed that the mechanist method could be used as a component of proving scientific discoveries. He simply questioned certain aspects of it, and to what extent it could be used. Most Christians then believed that God created the world in seven days and that it was forever unchanging. Newton proved otherwise. Since more and more advancements were being made in science, the monotheistic culture searched for some way to unite God and science. People, such as Richard Bentley, argued that Newton was the factor they needed for their unification. He actually became a "symbol

"One can go back toward safety or forward toward growth."
Abraham Maslow

of science in a Christian Society."[2]

In attempting to separate science from God, scientists of his time found it to be a challenging endeavor. Only so many questions could be answered. There was only so far science could go in explaining the universe. They could explain why the planets revolved around the sun, how the universe was expanding, and that a big bang probably started it all; however, they could not explain what caused it all to happen to begin with. Scientists knew how the universe was created, but they did not know why the universe existed. Science con-

> *Even if science explained how everything worked in the universe, they would never, no matter how many questions they answered, know what put the universe here to begin with. When they answered every question available to them, they would run into the wall. Beyond that wall was God.*

sisted of explaining known facts and categorizing them, not the initial creation of them. Even if science explained how everything worked in the universe, they would never, no matter how many questions they answered, know what put the universe here to begin with. When they answered every question available to them, they would run into the wall. Beyond that wall was God.

The acceptance that it was impossible to answer the overwhelming questions in the universe proved that something powerful and intelligent existed beyond their comprehension. Some intelligent Being calculated every minute detail in creating this universe. It ran too perfectly. Although it was constantly changing, it still ran in perfect order. This would make it rather difficult not to believe in a God or an

"Every one has an inner light that tells him what is proper. It has been called the law of God written on the heart."
Frederick Bailes,
Hidden Power for Human Problems.

intelligent Being. This was probably why so many physicists maintained a profound belief in God. It had to be understood within the context of the scientists' mind. They were using the absolute realities found in an awe-striking universe to prove God. Frederick Bailes, a spiritualist mentioned that a scientist once told him that he, once stopped, plucked a sweet pea, and remarked; "A chemist can make this fragrance synthetically. He can even tell to a certain degree the process by which the scent was developed in nature. A plastics operator can make a flower as beautiful as this.

> The theory of an expanding universe simply states that the universe is not static and unchanging; it is constantly expanding. The theory is that after the *big bang* caused the creation of the planets and stars, the galaxies and solar systems continue to move out from the center. They expand at a rate too fast for the gravitational force to pull them back. Newton claimed that he did not know what kept the planets from collapsing on each other, but that what *caused it* proved the existence of a God. In the same respect, we still have no clue why a ball of mass exploded and caused this phenomena.

But science cannot yet make a living sweet pea. My faith rests upon the fact that this flower has a matchless Maker."3

Newton proved the existence of gravity; however, he questioned what kept the planets and stars from collapsing in on each other because of the gravitational force. He concluded that God intervened to prevent this from happening. Actually, his theory is wrong, scientists have discovered now that planets and stars did not fall in on each other because of an

"Fear defeats more people that any other one thing in the world."
Ralph Waldo Emerson

expanding universe, but the principle of his point remains valid. The theory of an expanding universe simply states that the universe is not static and unchanging; it is constantly expanding. The theory is that after the *big bang* caused the creation of the planets and stars, the galaxies and solar systems continue to move out from the center. They expand at a rate too fast for the gravitational force to pull them back. Newton claimed that he did not know what kept the planets from collapsing on each other, but that what *caused* it proved the existence of a God. In the same respect, we still have no clue *why* a ball of mass exploded and caused this phenomena. Furthermore, not only do we not know what *causes* this phenomena, the universe constantly evolves and God constantly intervenes. Newton explained that the power of gravity maintained the order of the universe, but Newton had "not yet assigned the cause of this power....I have not been able to discover the causes of those properties of gravity from phenomena." He determined that the order of the universe proved God's existence, but also that science could explain the outcome or the effect of that order.[4]

The beautiful creation of such an orderly system of the universe "could only proceed from the counsel and dominion of an intelligent and powerful Being." Newton called this powerful being God.

Newton discovered gravity, and that centripetal force, a kind of gravity, caused matter to tend toward a center. The planets revolved around the sun "in circles concentric with the sun." Because of gravitational force it was impossible for all the matter of the planets and the stars "to fly up from them, and become evenly spread throughout all the heavens, without a supernatural power." What kept the matter of the planets from collapsing in on one another to form one great mass? Newton induced that the continual separation of the planets and stars in the universe "may all depend upon cer-

*"Human passions might be bind, unmeasured,
but they were not evil."*
Peter Gay,
The Party of Humanity.

tain forces by which the particles of bodies, by some causes hitherto unknown."5

Newton determined that God must intervene to force the planets to rotate around the sun. The motion of the planets was caused by the intervention of a voluntary agent; "diurnal rotation of the planets could not be derived from gravity, but required a divine arm to impress them." Newton concluded that; "it is not to be conceived that mechanical causes could give birth to so many regular motions, since the comets range overall parts of the heavens in very eccentric orbits." The beautiful creation of such an

*"Don't cling to reason so desperately
in a world of so many horrid
contradictions."*
Anne Rice, Pandora

orderly system of the universe "could only proceed
from the counsel and dominion of an intelligent and
powerful Being." Newton called this powerful being
God.[6]

In opposition to the predetermined interpretation
of the universe, Newton believed that God intervened

"Make visible what, without you, might perhaps never have been seen."
Robert Biessen

and was always present in the universe. This did not mean he thought God to be imperfect. The supreme God was "eternal, infinite, and absolutely perfect." After all, if he did not dominate all things, he could not be our God. God did not actually embody eternity, infinity, space, and time, but was a constant part of the universe by being eternal, infinite, and existing forever and always. Newton compared this theory to people; "Every soul that has perception is, though in different times and in different organs of sense and motion, still the same indivisible person." Just like people were always the same throughout their life, God was always the same God always and everywhere.7

"As a blind man has no idea of colors, so have we no idea of the manner by which the all-wise God perceives and understands all things;" Newton explained to show that science could prove an effect to something without being able to prove an underlying cause. Furthermore, he concluded that; "We know him only by his most wise and excellent contrivances of things and final causes." How could all these unbelievable causes within our universe be deduced to pure chance? Because of the impossibility of such a perfect universe running like clockwork by chance, Newton believed that it was absurd and senseless to be an atheist. During the seventeenth-century, atheism was "no longer just an individual standpoint but a philosophical school and genuine system of thought." Within the new mathematical and mechanical philosophy, the possibly of no God became a legitimate question.[8]

Newton inquired; "Did blind chance know that there was light and what was its refraction, and fit the eyes of all creatures after the most curious manner to make use it?"

Many proponents of the mechanical philosophy of the time did not believe in miracles because they were in violation of the laws of nature. Define the laws of nature? Does the earth appearing to spin on an axis because according to quantum theory it is situated within a time warp seem like a perfectly natural thing to happen by chance? Is the existence of gravity that holds people on earth not a miracle? Where did gravity come from? People know its there because of Newton, but how did it come into *existence*? If all

"Life is an opportunity, benefit from it.
Life is beauty, admire it.
Life is bliss, taste it.
Life is a dream, realize it.
Life is a challenge, meet it.
Life is a duty, complete it.
Life is a game, play it."

Mother Teresa

this was explainable by the laws of nature, what could not be? These things seemed more miraculous than what many were declaring to be miracles.

Newton inquired; "Did blind chance know that there was light and what was its refraction, and fit the eyes of all creatures after the most curious manner to make use it?" Furthermore, was it more probable that a God created a body that runs almost perfectly like a machine, enabled it to see, smell, hear, taste, and feel--both by touch and within themselves, and made the heart pump; or that by

chance some huge ball of dirt shattered making *by accident* a perfectly rotating solar system that would eventually allow molecules to come together and form perfectly structured beings? Scientists who insisted these perfectly operating things happen *by chance* always argued that people must realize how much time passed for these things to evolve. Time seemed to be there best excuse. They basically said that anything, no matter how absurd, could happen by accident given enough time.[9]

Newton's definition of a miracle is that; "it seems to me that the example of a Planet wch goes round and preserves it[s] motion in its Orb without any

other help but that of God, being compared wth a Planet kept in its Orb by yt matter wch constantly drives it toward ye sun, plainly shews what difference there is between natural and rational miracles."[10]

Proponents of Newton's philosophy believed God created the world only to naturally intervene to keep it running smoothly. Therefore, Newton's philosophy was the most grounded in sources of natural religion. The wisdom of God could be compared to a clockmaker making a clock "capable of going on without him... for that's impossible" since everything was dependent on God, but his wisdom relied on him "framing originally the perfect and complete idea of a work, which begun and continues according to that original perfect idea, by the continual uninterrupted exercise of his power."[11]

Newton did not suppose that God was the soul of the world, which was part of a compound within the body, but that he was a governor. The soul and body act upon each other, but God acted upon the universe even though the universe did not act upon him. He believed God existed everywhere at all times and was omniscient. Newton said that God was present in all places and could see everything, "as the mind of man is present to all the pictures of things formed in his brain."

Newton did not suppose that God was the soul of the world, which was part of a compound within the body, but that he was a governor. The soul and body act upon each other, but God acted upon the universe even though the universe did not act upon him. He believed God existed everywhere at all times and was omniscient. Newton said that God

was present in all places and could see everything, "as the mind of man is present to all the pictures of things formed in his brain."[12]

Scientists know now that the universe is expanding, therefore it is not static. That is why the stars do not collapse on each other as a result of gravitational force. This does not rule out divine intervention. The general theory of relativity states that the universe used to be a big ball of mass, until a big bang forced particles of matter to shoot out and expand, forming planets, stars, and galaxies. After the big bang, the universe did not become static. It continues to expand further and further out. One theory is that it will eventually re-collapse to form one great mass again. However, the speed that the universe travels in expanding is greater than the gravitational force and that keeps the planets and stars from falling in on each other. Steven Hawking asserted that; "At the big bang and other singularities, all the laws would have broken down, so God would still have had complete freedom to choose what happened and how the universe began."[13]

Further proof that the universe is continually changing came in the 1905, when Einstein published a paper of the theory of relativity denouncing the idea of absolute space and time. The development of quantum theory outdated Newton's theory of an ether substance in the air. Newton thought that ether encompassed all of space, and for that reason, the measurement of time was relative according to substance of ether it was traveling through. After Einstein disproved absolute time, there was need for the ether. All matter could now be measured using the speed of light, no matter how fast they were traveling, because nothing could travel faster than the speed of light.[14]

"Its reduction and tendency to over-simplification mean that mechanism is no longer a viable option for understanding nature;" Jones explained was the reason for the eventual denouncement of the mechanical philosophy. Scientists have

Steven Hawking asserted that;

"At the big bang and other singularities, all the laws would have broken down, so God would still have had complete freedom to choose what happened and how the universe began."

accepted that they cannot prove the cause of everything in the universe, and that there must be explainable reasons for scientific phenomena. Science cannot be reduced to a few simple rules, because "many of the laws that have been uncovered are not deterministic but contain elements of indeterminacy and contingency." Many physicists are open-minded to unexplainable reasons to natural causes; therefore, this leaves room for the emergence of a combination of science and God. Or, at least, the acceptance that parallels may exist between the two of them.[15]

With this chapter, I discussed Newton's Proof of God and why he believed science and God should be interdependent. In the next chapter, I examine Rousseau's belief that people should look to their soul and nature for peace and happiness, instead of relying entirely upon reason. He believed that within each of us lay a knowledge of morality, who we are and God.

Endnotes:

1 See James W. Jones, The Redemption of Matter: Towards the Repprochement of Science and Religion (Lanham: University Press of America, 1984), 66; Richard Popkin, "The Religious Background of Seventeenth-Century Philosophy," in The Cambridge History of Seventeenth-Century Philosophy, eds. Daniel Garber and Michael Ayers (Cambridge: Cambridge University Press, 1998), 393; and Steven Nadler, "Doctrines of Explaination in Late Scholasticism and in the Mechanical Philosophy," 513-536.

2 Frank E. Manuel, The Changing of the Gods (New York: Bantum Books, 1996), 15-16.

3 Frederick Bailes, Hidden Powers for Human Problems (Englewood Cliffs, NJ: Prentice-Hall, 1957), 38-39; and Isaac Newton, Newton's Philosophy of Nature: Selections From his Writings, with a Foreword by John Herman Randallm Jr., (New York: Hafner Press, 1953), 45.

4 Isaac Newton, Newton's Philosophy of Nature: Selections From his Writings, with a Foreword by John Herman Randallm Jr., (New York: Hafner Press, 1953), 45.

5 See Newton, Newton's Philosophy, 42, 47, & 57; and Isaac Newton, The Mathematical Principles of Natural Philosophy, with a Foreword by I. Bernard Cohen, (London: Dawsons of Pall Mall, 1968), 3.

6 See Newton, Mathematical Principles, 14; and Newton, Newton's Philosophy, 42 & 57.

7 Newton, Newton's Philosophy, 42-43.

8 See Newton, Newton's Philosophy, 44 & 65; and Jean-Robert Armogathe, "Proofs of the Existence of God," in Cambridge, 305.

9 Ibid., 66.

10 Rupert A. Hall and Laura Tilling, ed., The Correspondence of Isaac Newton, vol. 5 (Cambridge: Cambridge University Press, 1975), 299.

11 Ibid., 12-24.

12 Ibid., 12-17.

13 Stephen Hawking, The Illustrated A Brief History of Time (New York: Bantam Books, 1996), 232.

14 See Hawking, 27-30; and P. M. Harman, Energy, Force, And Matter: The Conceptual Development of Nineteenth-Century Physics (Cambridge: Cambridge University Press, 1982), 153-155.

15 Jones, 96.

Chapter 4:
Jean-Jacques Rousseau:
A Profession of Faith

"If we could be contented with being what we are, we should have no inducement to lament our fate; but we inflict on ourselves a thousand real evils in seeking after an imaginary happiness."
Jean Jacques Rousseau,
"Profession of Faith of a Savoyard Vicar"

Chapter 4:
Jean-Jacques Rousseau:
A Profession of Faith

*A*s a rebel of the enlightenment, Jean-Jacques Rousseau denounced the reasoning of the philosophes. Many philosohes subscribed to a rational moral belief based on natural law, while Rousseau focused on gut feelings before reason as the true source of morality. In the "Profession of Faith of a Savoyard Vicar," his "principles and faith which governed his life and conduct" are told through the mind of the Savoyard Vicar.[1]

"Nature, my dear youth, hath hitherto in this respect been silent to you," the Savoyard Vicar first explained to the young man whom he was professing his faith. Natural law of the universe governed his system of faith, all morality and truth could be discovered in nature.

Rousseau subscribed to the principle of an innate Supreme Being to acquire ultimate truth: "my innate instructor, who will deceive me less than I may be deceived by others." In examining the mind and body, he proclaims that; "A mere machine is evidently incapable of thinking,...whereas in man there exists something perpetually prone to expand." He combined his acquiescence of individualism with this theory that within everyone, an "innate sense of truth" exists and "I shall grow less depraved in the pursuit of my own illusions, than in giving myself up to the deceptions of others."[2]

Rousseau subscribed to the principle of an innate Supreme Being to acquire ultimate truth: "my innate instructor, who will deceive me less than I may be deceived by others."

After he determined that his mind was guided by an innate instructor, he concluded that he must exist because he possessed sensations. All sensations were internal but caused by external objects. Since external objects were free to act on their own and were not dependent another objects' actions, other objects must also exist. Everything that his senses acted upon, he called matter and parts of matter united to form individual beings. He may appear to be hinting toward elements of empiricism, but not quite. The traditional meaning of empiricism relies solely on sensations through external observation and experiment for proof, while Rousseau obtained ultimate proof from an innate instructor: "But when, delivered from the delusions of sense, we shall enjoy the contemplation of the Supreme Being, and those eternal truths of which he is the source."[3]

Furthermore, not only could people sense matter, but they could also judge it by intellectual comparison. Therefore, humans were intelligent active beings. His next determined that matter could encounter mechanical or spontaneous motion, but the cause of motion did not exist in matter. A *Will* gave it motion. From this he established his first article of faith; "a *Will* gives motion to the universe, and animates all nature." His argument was similar to Sir Isaac Newton's design argument in that the world did not move on its own, but some foreign agent governed its motion; "it is impossible for me to observe the apparent diurnal revolution of the sun, without conceiving that some force must urge it forward."[4]

"The world is governed by a wise and powerful

"The world is governed by a wise and powerful Will" was Rousseau's second article of faith. He went further to explain that the Being that "gives motion to all parts of the inverse, I call God."

"Do you run on ahead?-Do you do so as a herdsman? Or as an exception? A third possibility would be as a deserter....First question of conscience."
Friedrich Nietzsche,
Twilight of the Idols

Will" was Rousseau's second article of faith. He went further to explain that the Being that "gives motion to all parts of the inverse, I call God." He resolved that he knew that God existed because he could feel him, and that his existence was dependent on God. Rousseau's intellectual judgment of his surroundings determined his will; moreover, he believed; "my will is independent of my senses, I can either consent to, or resist their impressions." In Summary, he believed a divine Will intellectually guided the universe and humans possessed the power and judgment to control their own will.[5]

If humans maintained power over their own will, then they must be free agents was his third article of faith; "If man be an active and free being, he acts of himself." Humans could choose to live a

> "We are in vain forbidden
> to do this thing or the other-
> -we shall feel but
> little remorse for
> doing anything to which
> a well-regulated natural
> instinct excites us,
> how strongly soever
> prohibited by reason."
>
> Jean-Jacques Rousseau

good and honest life or a bad one, whatever they chose would not affect the natural order of the universe. Furthermore, if people chose the evil path, they would live in an unavoidable hell on earth. However, he held a deterministic belief of free-will given only by the power of God; "we are free only because it is His will that we should be so."[6]

Nature would not allow people to suffer, it was simply what they chose by succumbing to temptations; "moral evil is incontestibly our own work." However he found within himself his own sense of innate morality; "We are in vain forbidden to do this thing or the other--we shall feel but little remorse for doing anything to which a well-regulated natural instinct excites us, how strongly soever prohibited by reason." He believed all people to be innately good and just, but they needed to resort to their conscience for guidance. "Be just and thou wilt be happy;" Rousseau professes that these words were written on his soul. An everlasting hell did not exist in his eyes; and furthermore, he inquired; "Where is the necessity

"Interested by a natural affinity
in favor of the young fugitive,
he examined very carefully
into his character and disposition.
In this examination,
he saw that his misfortunes
had already debased his heart,
--that the shame and contempt
to which he had been exposed
had depressed his ambition,
and that his disappointed pride,
converted into indignation,
had deduced,
from the injustice and cruelty
of mankind, the depravity of
human nature and the emptiness of virtue.
He had observed religion
made use of a mask to self-interest,
and its worship as a cloak to hypocrisy."

Jean-Jacques Rousseau,
"Profession of Faith of a Savoyard Vicar"

of seeking a hell in another life, when it is to be found even in this,--in the hearts of the wicked." True happiness could be acquired by desiring it in others.7

"I have only to consult myself concerning what I ought to do. All that I feel to be right, is right;" were his foundations for nineteenth-century Romanticism and individualism that concentrated on searching within ourselves first for answers instead of only relying on reason. He stated that "reason deceives us but too often, and has given us a right to distrust her conclusions; but conscience never deceives us." Within the conscience existed an "innate principle of justice and goodness." He believed that "conscience was the voice of the soul,--the passions are the voice of the body."[8]

Society should reach "an enlightened mode of worship," Rousseau concluded while explaining that all religions should retain certain elements of natu-

> "Laziness and cowardice
> are the reasons why so
> great a portion of mankind,
> after nature has long since discharged
> them from external direction,
> nevertheless remain under
> lifelong tutelage,
> and why it is so easy for others
> to set themselves up
> as their guardians."
>
> Immanuel Kant,
> "What is Enlightenment?"

ral religion. He believed people could find God within themselves with no need of other worship. If people observed nature and listened to their voice within, then God would give them conscience and understanding. "The God whom I adore is not a God of darkness; he hath not given me an understanding to forbid me the use of it," described the foundations of his religious belief. Many religions encompassed the world, but everyone believed other religions were absurd. He believed more

than one path existed to salvation. Religions and their teachings changed greatly over time, yet people held so dearly to their current doctrines.[9]

Lastly, he concluded that people should primarily look at nature to find the answers. He believed

> *"The book of nature lies open to every eye. It is from this sublime and wonderful volume that I learn to serve and adore its Divine Author. No person is excusable for neglecting to read this book, as it is written in an universal language, intelligible to all mankind."*
>
> *Jean-Jacques Rousseau*

that what was eternal was beyond him; "But I know that God hath formed the universe and all that exists, in the most consummate order. He is doubtless eternal, but I am incapacitated to conceive an idea of eternity. Why then should I amuse myself with words?" Within nature existed the only universal language that is intelligible to society; "I could never believe that God required me, under pain of eternal damnation, to

"Are you genuine? Or only an actor? A representative? Or that itself which is represented?-Finally you are no more than an imitation of an actor....Second question of conscience."
Friedrich Nietzsche,
Twilight of the Idols

be so very learned; and, therefore, I shut up all my books." And instead, he trusts his heart. And finally he surmises that; "The book of nature lies open to every eye. It is from this sublime and wonderful volume that I learn to serve and adore its Divine Author. No person

is excusable for neglecting to read this book, as it is written in an universal language, intelligible to all mankind."[10]

Endnotes:

1 Jean-Jacques Rousseau, The Harvard Classics: French and English Philosopher, "Profession of Faith of the Savoyard Vicar, (New York: P. F. Collier, 1910), 237.

2 Ibid, 243 & 259.

3 Ibid, 264.

4 Ibid, 249.

5 Ibid, 254 & 259.

6 Ibid, 260 & 266.

7 Ibid, 239, 261 & 265.

8 Ibid, 268 &272.

9 Ibid, 289.

10 Ibid, 267 & 300.

A Conclusion

"Always be a first-rate version of yourself, instead of a second-rate version of someone else."
Judy Garland

A Conclusion

*I*n this book I examined our soul and theories of where our soul comes from. Searching for happiness and contentment within our selves enables us to want happiness for others. We become happy with our selves when we get to know our selves, because we are no longer neglecting our inner self. If you're happy, you want others to be happy. If you look in your soul and find your true self, then you can get to know yourself and become happy with yourself. When you get to know yourself, you see that all people have flaws, but you can strive to be the best person you can be. You become happy with what you have today, while also looking forward to the future. You find good passion in all areas of

your life, because when you get to know yourself the world becomes more exciting. And you discover a deeper happiness within yourself. This is because when you find yourself, you acquire a better understanding of yourself and the world around you. And finally by accepting yourself, you create a life for yourself that represents what you truly desire in life.

As you get to know yourself, you will learn to see the world through your soul; which helps you see what is most important, such as love, family, and loved ones. You will understand that all people make mistakes or may do things you do not understand, but what's impor-

tant is that they have a good heart. And you will be less
tempted to judge people based their race, religion, culture or socio-economic status. By viewing the world
from your soul, you will see that money alone will never
make you happy; but by knowing yourself you will find
happiness with the world and yourself. And with that
knowledge of yourself, you will have a key to understanding the world around you in a whole new light.

Remember to trust your instincts. There is a communication beyond words or our language within you; it is a communication from God, the universe, and nature. And by doing this, you will not only find a deep peace and happiness within yourself, but also with the world. Life is a gift, let's go out and live it.

Reader's Questions

for

What is Enlightenment:
Theories of Plato, Newton, Rousseau and
Kant on Knowing Yourself beneath Your
Societal Identity, God and
the Unseen Realm

1. How would you describe your true self
beneath your societal identity?

2. What is the most captivating quality
about you?

3. What are your beliefs about the intelligence throughout the universe?

4. Who is your favorite philosopher?
What is it about that person that makes
her or him your favorite?

Works Cited:

Bailes, Frederick; *Hidden Power for Human Problems.*

Gay, Peter; *The Party of Humanity.*

Hawking, Stephen; *The Illustrated A Brief History of Time.*

Kant, Immanuel; *Basic Writings of Kant.*

Kant, Immanuel; *Critique of Pure Reason.*

Kant, Immanuel; "What is Enlightenment?"

Leakey, Richard; *The Origin of Humankind.*

Newton, Isaac; *Newton's Philosophy of Nature.*

Newton, Isaac; *The Mathematical Principles of Natural Philosophy.*

Nietzsche, Friedrich; *Twilight of the Idols.*

Plato; *A Guided Tour of Five Works by Plato.*

Rousseau, Jean-Jacques; "Profession of Faith of a Savoyard Vicar," from *Emile: On Education.*

About the Author

K.J. Cleveland was born in Alabama, grew up in various areas, including Mannheim, Germany, due to her Mom being a librarian for the U.S. Army. Her mother, Sherrie Floyd, opened libraries for the U.S. Army in Bosnia, and subsequently won Federal Librarian of the Year in 2001 for her endeavors. K.J. Cleveland has a Bachelor's Degree in psychology and a Master's Degree in history with concentrations in philosophy. After college, she moved to California, where she began her writing career. She and her brother, Randy Jones, published *The Raw You: Self-Awareness Journal* for one year in West Los Angeles, followed by a book, *The Raw You: A Contemplation of the Soul*, which received an incredibly positive response from its readers. Other books she has written include *The Courage to be Yourself: Look Inside and Develop the Confidence to be Your True Self, What is Enlightenment? Theories about God and the Unseen Realm, and Knowing Yourself Beneath Your Societal Identity From Plato, Isaac Newton, Jean-Jacques Rousseau and Immanuel Kant* and *Never Give Up: Exercises to Listen to Your Heart, Set Goals and Make Your Dreams Come True.* To learn more about knowing yourself and making your dreams come true, check out www.ToKnowThyself.org, www.NeverGiveUp1.com, www.DreamsComeTrue1.org and www.WhatIsEnlightenment1.org.

Also by

K.J. Cleveland

The Courage to be Yourself: Look Inside and Develop the Confidence to be Your True Self

This book offers information on becoming yourself, who you are meant to be. In this book you will find information and exercises to help you discover who you really are and who you really want to be, and to help you develop the confidence to be that person.

Never Give Up: Exercises to Listen to Your Heart, Set Goals and Make Your Dreams Come True

Never give up on what you really want in life. When you make your dreams a reality they help you expand your awareness and grow as an individual. This book helps you uncover your true dreams in life, and offers goal-setting exercises to help you never give up on your dreams and make them come true.

Never Give Up:
Exercises to Listen to Your Heart, Set Goals and Make Your Dreams Come True

by K.J. Cleveland

No matter our age, we all have inherent dreams and desires we would like to see come forth in our lives. Our dreams are what we are put on earth to do. Sometimes, however, we unconsciously limit ourselves without even knowing it. We may try to live up to the standards we feel society has set for us, and if those images are not in line with our dreams, we consequently banish our deepest desires.

When you make your dreams a reality they help you expand your awareness and grow as an individual. This book helps you uncover your true dreams in life, and offers goal-setting exercises to help you never give up on your dreams and make them come true.

Never give up on what you really want in life. Let these exercises motivate you to stick to your goals and make your dreams come true. Throughout the book are examples of people who never gave up on their dreams, I hope their stories inspire and motivate you.

"The way to get started is to quit talking and begin doing."
-Walt Disney

"Some people buy into the philosophy that you have a few good years before the next generation comes along and tells you to step aside. Don't believe that. The older we get, the smarter we get and the smarter we live. You can achieve extraordinary things in your fifties, seventies, and beyond if you really want to."
-Sylvester Stallone

Made in the USA
San Bernardino, CA
25 May 2013